Jesus and Entrepreneurship

Biblical Foundations for Success

Table of Contents

1. Introduction 1

2. Entrepreneurial Lessons from Jesus 2

3. Biblical Wisdom: A Guide for Modern Entrepreneurs 5

    3.1. A New Look at Ancient Wisdom 5

    3.2. Resilience in the Face of Adversity 6

    3.3. Practicing Servant Leadership 6

    3.4. Principle of Sowing and Reaping 7

    3.5. The Power of Purpose 7

4. The Parable of the Talents: Investing and Risk-Taking 9

    4.1. The Parable: An Overview 9

    4.2. Investment: An Essential Tool for Growth 10

    4.3. Risk: An Integral Part of the entrepreneurial journey 10

    4.4. Consequence management: Preparing for outcomes 11

    4.5. The Master-Servant Relationship: Leaders and their Teams . 11

5. 'Blessed are the Meek': Embracing Humility in Leadership 13

    5.1. Humility: An Undervalued Virtue 13

    5.2. Embracing Humility for Effective Leadership 14

    5.3. Servant Leadership: Harnessing Power through Humility . . . 14

6. Modeling Jesus' Humility in Entrepreneurship 15

7. In Conclusion: Transforming Leadership Paradigms 16

8. Jesus as a Servant Leader: The Ultimate Role Model 17

    8.1. The Concept of Servant Leadership 17

    8.2. Servant Leadership in Entrepreneurship 18

    8.3. Jesus' Teachings as Actionable Strategies 18

    8.4. Implementing Servant Leadership 19

    8.5. Conclusion 20

9. 'Faith as a Mustard Seed': Building Businesses from Humble

Beginnings 21

9.1. The Metamorphosis of the Mustard Seed ... 21

9.2. The Power of Patience and Perseverance ... 22

9.3. Nurture Your Seed: Developing Your Vision ... 22

9.4. A Safe Haven for Many: The Larger Purpose ... 23

9.5. A Leap of Faith: Trusting the Divine Plan ... 23

10. The Loaves and Fishes: Maximizing Limited Resources ... 25

10.1. Understanding the Parable ... 25

10.2. Key Entrepreneurial Lessons ... 25

10.3. Implementing the Lessons ... 27

10.4. Maximise Existing Resources ... 27

10.5. Foster a Culture of Innovation ... 27

10.6. Build a Community ... 27

10.7. Embrace Abundance ... 27

11. Jesus and Communication: Creating Impactful Interactions ... 29

11.1. The Basis of Successful Communication: Love and Respect ... 29

11.2. Listening: A Forgotten Skill ... 29

11.3. Parables: Art of Storytelling ... 30

11.4. The Power of Questions ... 30

11.5. Clarity and Simplicity ... 30

11.6. Non-Verbal Communication ... 31

11.7. The Authenticity Factor ... 31

12. Gethsemane and Passion: Resilience in the Face of Challenges ... 32

12.1. The Garden in Context ... 32

12.2. Resilience: A Biblical Perspective ... 33

12.3. Demonstrating Resilience in Business ... 33

12.4. Faith and Resilience ... 34

12.5. Application for the Modern Entrepreneur ... 34

13. The Resurrection: Turning Failure into Success ... 36

13.1. Trading Defeat for Victory ... 36

13.2. The Power of Resilience ... 37

13.3. Reframing Failure 37

13.4. Ethical Leadership 38

Chapter 1. Introduction

Delve into the heartening world of spirituality mingled with entrepreneurial wisdom with our special report: "Jesus and Entrepreneurship: Biblical Foundations for Success". This report elegantly intertwines age-old biblical teachings with contemporary business wisdom, offering refreshing perspectives to growth, leadership, and success in entrepreneurship. Walking through the pages, you'll uncover riveting narratives where the life and teachings of Jesus Christ provide actionable insights for entrepreneurs today. This isn't just another business manual, it's a vibrant blend of faith and commerce that celebrates personal growth, guides ethical decisions, and illuminates the path to purposeful success. Let your entrepreneurial spirit be touched by the timeless wisdom of biblical teachings and prepare for an enlightening journey which might just transform the way you see your business, and your role within it!

Chapter 2. Entrepreneurial Lessons from Jesus

When scanning the Scripture's vast narratives and teachings, several principles and valuable lessons emerge, particularly applicable for the entrepreneurial world. These principles aren't merely about morality or righteousness; they comprise guidelines for leadership, relationships, adversity handling, and risk-management - elements that are inextricably linked with entrepreneurship.

=== The Parable of Talents: Understanding Assets and Risks

Drawn from the Gospel of Matthew (25:14-30), the Parable of Talents reflects the essence of risks and assets in entrepreneurship. As per the story, a master, traveling abroad, entrusted his three servants with 'talents' or various valuable measures—five to the first, two to the second, and a single talent to the third.

Upon his return, the master discovered distinct outcomes. The first two servants had bravely taken risks and had invested their talents, doubling the resources. Rewarding them for their entrepreneurial spirit, for they had shown a keen understanding of asset allocation and risk-taking, he entrusted them with greater responsibilities.

On the other hand, the third servant, bound by fear, safeguarded his talent by burying it. Upon his master's return, he handed back the single talent untouched. This servant, representing the fear-driven entrepreneur, was rebuked by the master for his inactivity and unprofitability.

Interpreting this parable, we must acknowledge the importance of understanding and wisely utilizing our resources and the courage of taking calculated risks in entrepreneurship. Underutilized resources and buried potentials limit the growth and development of a business.

=== Building on The Foundation: Prioritizing Sustainability Upon Growth

The parables of the wise and foolish builders, found in Matthew 7:24-27, exhorts the importance of building a solid, unshakable foundation. The wise builder who constructs his house on rock symbolizes leadership that prioritizes robust, ethical foundations over rapid, unstable growth. When the storms and winds (unforeseen challenges in business) come, the house remains standing firm.

In contrast, the foolish builder opts for a seemingly convenient choice—building his house on sand. Despite its initial appearance of quick progress and success, the house inevitably collapses under the storm's pressures. This signifies the potential downfall of businesses built on shaky grounds without a strong moral and business foundation.

The wise builder denotes a wise entrepreneur—one who is undeterred by the allure of quick successes, rigidly adheres to ethics, and persistently strives to maintain a resilient business framework before expanding.

=== The Good Shepherd: Leading with Compassion and Responsibility

Jesus' portrayal as the Good Shepherd, in John 10:11-18, holds profound implications for entrepreneurial leadership. Jesus, as the Good Shepherd, is portrayed as a leader who knows each of his sheep individually, cares for them, and is willing to sacrifice for their well-being.

This image resonates deeply with how leaders should perceive their team. Leaders shouldn't merely view their teammates as resources or employees but should strive to know and understand them individually, take care of their needs, and safeguard their interests—even at personal cost. The Good Shepherd leadership stresses empathy, responsibility, and selflessness as core to leading successfully in an entrepreneurial context.

=== The Mustard Seed: Patience and Organic Growth

The Parable of the Mustard Seed (Matthew 13:31-32) emphasizes the value of patience and faith in organic growth. The mustard seed, one of the smallest of all seeds, grows into a large tree, providing a haven for birds to perch in its branches.

This tale becomes a metaphor for how an idea, as tiny as a mustard seed, can grow into something meaningful and impactful given the right nurturing. Hence, as entrepreneurs, we should not be disheartened by small beginnings or be impatient for quick results. Rather, we should trust the process of organic growth and concentrate on nurturing our ideas until they eventually yield results.

Jesus' teachings and life provide an abundance of strategic wisdom, framed in a spiritual context. Applying these lessons genuinely can infuse our entrepreneurial journey with hope, inspiration, and success. Yet, the journey, though promising, is rarely smooth. It requires faith, resilience, humility, patience, and a continuous commitment to growth and learning. But more than anything, it demands the courage to accept and implement these lessons sincerely in our entrepreneurial lives. By doing so, we take on the challenge of shaping not just successful businesses, but also meaningful lives that reflect the very wisdom that guides us.

Chapter 3. Biblical Wisdom: A Guide for Modern Entrepreneurs

In the bustling marketplace of modern entrepreneurship, there exists a timeless compass, a guiding beacon that often goes unnoticed - the wisdom traced in the Bible. This anthology of sacred teachings, imparted by the exemplar of selflessness and leadership, Jesus Christ, might appear distilled in the folds of spirituality, but when observed through the lens of a discerning entrepreneur, unfolds rich insights and practical advice that bear relevance even today.

3.1. A New Look at Ancient Wisdom

Many entrepreneurs associate their success with innovative ideas or financial strategy, often overlooking the influence their inner values and principles can make. The Bible, housing an enduring source of moral guidance and character building, can hold remarkable insights for individuals navigating the minefield of entrepreneurship. The teachings of Jesus notably favor humility, service, resilience, and long-term vision, features that remarkably align with modern business wisdom.

In the Sermon on the Mount, Jesus profoundly stated, "Blessed are the meek, for they will inherit the earth" (Matthew 5:5). This statement prizes humility, a quality which countless entrepreneurs have found to be a catalyst for growth. This humility allows entrepreneurs to accept their limitations, learn from their mistakes, and to value the contributions of others in their journey.

3.2. Resilience in the Face of Adversity

Failures and setbacks are unavoidable in the world of entrepreneurship. The parable of the Sower (Matthew 13: 1-9), which talks about a sower who scattered seeds on different types of soil, provides a powerful metaphor for entrepreneurs. The seeds falling on rocky grounds initially sprout but later wither away, symbolizing ideas or ventures that collapse under the strain of hardship or criticism.

The key takeaway for entrepreneurs is to foster resilience. Business ideas must be rooted deeply with thorough research, planning, and a robust business model. Only then they can survive the inevitable challenges and grow to bear fruit.

3.3. Practicing Servant Leadership

One of the key philosophies Jesus propagated was the concept of servant leadership, as indicated by his words, "Instead, whoever wants to become great among you must be your servant" (Matthew 20:26). This approach sees the leader's primary role as serving their team, focusing on their growth, and creating an environment that nurtures both personal and professional development.

In the world of entrepreneurship, this translates into creating a company culture that celebrates each team member's contributions, bolsters a collaborative atmosphere, and encourages intellectual curiosity. When employees feel valued and empowered, the result is not just a successful business, but an organization that improves lives and makes a positive impact.

3.4. Principle of Sowing and Reaping

Another biblical lesson witnessed in Galatians 6:7 - "A man reaps what he sows" - holds ubiquitous relevance in entrepreneurship. It underscores that the outcomes we experience are directly tied to the actions we commit.

In the entrepreneurial context, the quality of the product or service, the attention to customer satisfaction, social responsibility, and ethical business practices, are all seeds sown that determine the success of the venture. In a world increasingly conscious of ethical consumption, responsible and purpose-driven businesses align perfectly with this principle.

3.5. The Power of Purpose

Jesus's life was a testament to living purposefully. His mission was to spread love, peace, and goodwill among humanity. He faced unimaginable trials, all faced with unwavering decisiveness and absolute surrender to his divine purpose.

Inspiration can be drawn by entrepreneurs to develop a clear, defined purpose for their businesses. It's not enough to only think about profit margins; one must consider the tangible difference their business will make in society. A purpose-driven business fosters loyalty among employees and consumers alike and augments the longevity of the business.

Entrepreneurship thrives when one negotiates the vast oceans of uncertainty, adapting to storms and swiftly catching winds of opportunity in one's sails. The Bible, when seen as a model for leadership, a source of wisdom that transcends years, cultures, and shifts in economic trends, proves to be an invaluable tool for entrepreneurs willing to learn from the teachings of Jesus. Faith, resilience, humility, and purpose distilled from His life can equip entrepreneurs with a moral compass and a guide to ethical success. Yes, entrepreneurship can often be a daunting journey, but when navigated with biblical wisdom, it not only enriches the business landscape but also the deeper strata of personal development and spiritual growth.

Chapter 4. The Parable of the Talents: Investing and Risk-Taking

It's challenging to consider a context that is more fitting for the discourse of entrepreneurship than that of 'The Parable of the Talents', one of the most renowned parables spoken by Jesus Christ. The parable weaves a story of a master who entrusts his servants with his property before embarking on a journey. It underscores the importance of investing resources and embracing risk, admonishing inaction and fear-driven conformity. The entrepreneurial relevance of this biblical story could not be more resolute.

4.1. The Parable: An Overview

Unveiling in Matthew 25:14-30 of the New Testament, the parable narrates how a master, before setting off on a journey, delegates his wealth amongst three of his servants. To one, he gives five talents, to another, two, and to the final servant, a mere one talent, each according to his individual ability. The servants that received five and two talents respectively invest and manage to double their offerings. The servant given one talent, fearing the wrath of the master, buries his share to prevent loss.

Upon return, the master praises the two fruitful servants for their loyal and effective stewardship. Yet, he reprimands the third servant, stripping him of his single talent and casting him into the 'outer darkness'.

4.2. Investment: An Essential Tool for Growth

The first spiritual lesson we draw from the parable revolves around the principle of investment. Investment, armed with patience and determination, leads to significant return over time. This echoes in the realm of entrepreneurship, where capital, time, and efforts must be diligently bestowed upon ideation, innovation, and growth. When the first two servants received their talents from their master, they immediately got to work. They invested wisely, reaped profits, and in doing so, received commendation and an invitation to enter into their master's happiness.

An entrepreneur investing in their business is akin to those servants - they, too, expect their investments, whether financial, temporal, or otherwise, to produce notable returns over time.

4.3. Risk: An Integral Part of the entrepreneurial journey

The Parable of the Talents also sheds light on the perception of risk and uncertainty. The third servant is constrained by fear, leading him to bury his talent in the ground. His fear of failure and punishment nudges him towards inaction, prompting disappointment from the master upon his return. This servant's attitude remarkably mirrors those entrepreneurs who are averse to risk-taking.

In entrepreneurship, risk and reward often go hand in hand – embarking on the journey of beginning a business involves steep risks. The fear of failure – of losing money or falling short of expectations, can be crippling. However, the parable reminds us that while risk is inherent, its presence doesn't call for inaction. Entrepreneurs, similar to the first two servants, must strive to analyse, assess, and address these risks strategically, while making the most of the resources at their disposal.

4.4. Consequence management: Preparing for outcomes

Additionally, the parable emphasizes the imperative nature of entrepreneurial foresight. The third servant, with his prophetic fear, did foresee an outcome: the master's scorn if he lost the talent. However, his approach to managing the potential consequence was driven by fear and myopia, which eventually led to the outcome he dreaded.

For entrepreneurs, this aspect of the parable underlines that not only is it essential to foresee possible outcomes, but we must also engage in effective consequence management.

Entrepreneurs, steady in their risk-taking, must also be prudent to design fallback plans. It's essential to realize that not all ventures will bear fruit and that setbacks are part and parcel of the entrepreneurial journey. Being prepared for potential negative outcomes can foster resilience and flexibility and help entrepreneurs rebound quickly from failure.

4.5. The Master-Servant Relationship: Leaders and their Teams

The interaction between the master and his servants serves as a metaphor for relationships between business leaders and their teams. The master entrusts his servants with great responsibilities and expects them to act as proper stewards.

This speaks directly to the entrepreneurial leader who delegates roles and responsibilities to their team members. Just like the master, they expect the team to not only fulfill their roles but to go above and beyond, to innovate, and deliver results

Effective, successful leaders understand this dynamic and fulfill their part in enabling their teams, fostering an environment of trust, and offering adequate mentorship.

The Parable of the Talents, while age-old, is still contemporary at its core. It expresses beliefs and guidelines that entrepreneurs can incorporate into their ventures, offering eternal wisdom on investment, risk-taking, consequence management, and leadership. Through this discourse, we see a testament that the entrepreneurial spirit is not just a modern phenomenon but an intrinsic aspect of our history. The stories may vary, the players may change, but the fundamental principles enabling success remain constant.

Chapter 5. 'Blessed are the Meek': Embracing Humility in Leadership

Humility, often misconstrued as timidity or lack of confidence, is primarily the essence of recognizing our human limitations. This recognition, however, doesn't hinder progress but in fact avidly fuels creativity, inclusivity, and the pursuit of sustainable success. The biblical instruction 'Blessed are the meek, for they shall inherit the earth' in Matthew 5:5, is a monumental teaching that provides transformative insights into effective leadership and business management.

5.1. Humility: An Undervalued Virtue

Humility is highly underappreciated as a virtue, especially in the world of business. Leadership is frequently associated with charismatic individuals exuding confidence and power. However, humility, an attitudinal quality marked by modesty and respect towards others' perspectives, plays a critical role in establishing potent leadership.

Humility in leadership might seem counterintuitive, especially in the context of secular definitions of leadership comprising dominance, competitiveness, and assertiveness. However, lessons from biblical teachings prompt leaders to recognize the importance of meekness.

Jesus, throughout his life, epitomized the virtue of humility. Despite being a revered religious figure, he often described himself as a servant, exemplifying humility in the grand scheme of leadership. He washed the feet of his disciples (John 13:1-17), a task typically reserved for the lowest of servants, demonstrating that no act of service was beneath him. This Jesus' act illustrates humble leadership—a leadership style that appeals to modern entrepreneurs.

5.2. Embracing Humility for Effective Leadership

A leadership approach rooted in humility fosters an organizational climate that encourages open dialogue, values diverse perspectives, nurtures learning, and cultivates a culture of respect.

Moreover, humble leaders don't have an overblown sense of their importance. They deeply appreciate their team players' views and are open to new ideas, promoting creativity and togetherness. Such a leader's grace and genuineness generate robust team morale, boosting productivity and promoting a healthy workplace environment.

5.3. Servant Leadership: Harnessing Power through Humility

The concept of servant leadership, embodied by Jesus, is a holistic approach to leadership that invests in individual growth while fostering a sense of community within the organization. Placing others' needs before one's own is at the core of servant leadership—a notion parallel to the beatitude 'Blessed are the meek'. A servant leader seeks to engender a sense of trust, collaboration, and the enlightenment of team members, allowing them to evolve into the best versions of themselves

Chapter 6. Modeling Jesus' Humility in Entrepreneurship

For entrepreneurs, embracing humility as demonstrated by Jesus, implies leading by serving. It's not about flexing one's influence or authority, but about leveraging these to serve others and make a difference. An entrepreneur's humility could translate into the following:

-. Listening Intently: Actively listening to team members, investors, partners, and even competitors to gain deep insights. -. Being Teachable: Showing willingness to continuously learn, unlearn, and relearn. Keeping oneself updated with the latest market trends and entrepreneurial theories. -. Recognizing Others: A humble leader credits the team for successes and owns up to failures. Celebrating achievements of the team, promotes a positive work environment. -. Soliciting Feedback: Inviting constructive feedback opens avenues for improvement, thereby enhancing the leader's effectiveness and the entrepreneurial venture's success. -. Seeking Guidance: A humble entrepreneur is not averse to seeking advice or mentorship, recognizing the value of guidance in steering the business effectively.

Chapter 7. In Conclusion: Transforming Leadership Paradigms

Humility, far from being a sign of weakness, is a force that transforms leadership paradigms for better. Jesus taught, through his life and actions, that humble leaders are indeed blessed. For entrepreneurs, this teaching sheds light on a leadership style marked by servitude, empathy, respect, and modesty—traits that go against the conventional notion of leadership that prizes dominance and competitiveness.

The business world, marked by volatility and disruption, requires leaders who can take a step back and recognize their limitations while learning from others. It needs more humble leaders who are patient listeners, lifelong learners, and respecters of diverse views and perspectives.

By espousing humility, entrepreneurs empower their teams, fuel business innovation, foster a healthy organizational culture, and, in the process, orient their ventures towards sustainable success. Indeed, 'Blessed are the meek...'.

Chapter 8. Jesus as a Servant Leader: The Ultimate Role Model

In this relentless pursuit of entrepreneurship, it becomes imperative to emulate those who demonstrated exceptional leadership traits. None better than Jesus Christ contrived an archetype of servant leadership that continues to inspire and guide countless around the globe. His leadership approach was not just about gaining followers, rather equipping them with knowledge, skills, and wisdom to become leaders themselves. The teachings, if understood and implemented in the entrepreneurial framework, hold tremendous potential to drive sustainable growth, build a high-performance culture, and foster harmonious relationships.

8.1. The Concept of Servant Leadership

In its simplest form, servant leadership refers to a leadership philosophy where the primary goal of the leader is to serve. This is different from traditional leadership where the leader's main focus is to drive the organization's growth. Servant leadership flips this definition, placing those who are being led as the primary concern.

Before entrepreneurial success steps in, one must first desire, as Jesus did, to serve those around. The journey starts by acknowledging that those around you are worth your time, attention, and utmost devotion. This approach fosters an environment of mutual respect and trust where everyone feels valued and integral to the organization's vision.

The biblical example of Jesus washing the feet of his disciples in John

13:1-17 exemplifies the essence of servant leadership. He humbly acted on the words, "The greatest among you will be your servant" (Matthew 23:11). Even being the leader, He took on a role usually reserved for the lowest of servants, embodying humility and selflessness that's at the heart of servant leadership.

8.2. Servant Leadership in Entrepreneurship

Translating this concept into entrepreneurship engages an emphasis on employee welfare, collaboration, empathy, and moral responsibility. This does not mean entrepreneurs should quite literally wash their employees' feet. The act signifies bending down to the level of the people, understanding their concerns, appreciating their efforts, and boosting their morale.

The simplest act of conveying gratitude can do wonders in fostering a vibrant work culture where people feel motivated to put their best foot forward. Servant leadership in entrepreneurship also means fostering an environment conducive to risk-taking, experimentation, and learning from failures – an indispensable attribute of thriving entrepreneurial settings.

Firms driven by servant leaders tend to demonstrate increased trust, greater engagement, higher productivity, and more inventive solutions. Employees feel heard, supported, and developed. They aspire to grow not just professionally but personally too under the impact of such leadership.

8.3. Jesus' Teachings as Actionable Strategies

By studying Jesus' life and teachings, entrepreneurs can derive actionable strategies that can navigate their entrepreneurial journey towards success. More than success, these teachings promise an understanding of fulfilling leadership and a profound influence that transcends the realm of work.

Jesus demonstrated that a leader's role is more than just about making decisions or strategizing; it's about staying committed to the group's betterment. He saw himself in others and shared in their joys and struggles. This empathy built a strong connection with his followers and enriched their faith in his leadership. Similarly, entrepreneurs should strive for an empathetic connection with their teams, making them feel understood and valued.

Jesus also propagated the concept of 'forgiveness', crucial in maintaining a healthy entrepreneurial ecosystem. Mistakes are common in any business setup. A forgiving and understanding leader instills confidence in the employees, encouraging a culture where learning thrives from each failure.

One of the recurring themes in Jesus's teachings is 'humility'. Time and again, Jesus emphasized being humble despite the powers He possessed. For an entrepreneur, this humility can reflect in being willing to accept criticism, learn from their own and others' mistakes, or acknowledge the team's contribution whenever the company achieves success.

8.4. Implementing Servant Leadership

Jesus' life provides a profound narrative on servant leadership. Entrepreneurs desiring to replicate these values need to introspect and possibly unlearn some traditional entrepreneurial norms. The focus should shift from 'Me' to 'We'. By prioritizing the needs of their team, promoting a culture of trust, and building a collaborative environment, entrepreneurs can support and enhance the collective abilities of their teams.

Moreover, practical servant leadership requires patience and relentless commitment as transformations do not happen overnight. It demands critical self-evaluation and constant learning. Entrepreneurs should be willing to accept that they don't have all the answers and should be open to learning from their employees.

8.5. Conclusion

In sum, Jesus's life offers a timeless model of servant leadership that, when applied within the entrepreneurial setup, can lead not only to business growth but also to wholesome personal development of everyone associated. This approach nurtures a vibrant entrepreneurial culture of trust, respect, empathy, and collaboration.

Ultimately, it is the aspiring vision of Jesus, a vision where everyone is nurtured and guided to take up the mantle of leadership themselves, that makes Him the ideal role model for entrepreneurs striving to make their mark in today's business world. This spiritual wisdom can truly form the bedrock for ethical and purposeful entrepreneurship.

Chapter 9. 'Faith as a Mustard Seed': Building Businesses from Humble Beginnings

In the gospel of Matthew (13:31-32), Jesus presents the parable of the mustard seed—the smallest of all seeds, yet when it grows, it is the largest of garden plants and becomes a tree so that the birds come and perch in its branches. It is this understanding that provides profound insight for entrepreneurs, illuminating the truth that gargantuan successes often come from the most modest beginnings.

9.1. The Metamorphosis of the Mustard Seed

The first and perhaps the most critical lesson of this parable is the transformative power of gradual growth. Much like the mustard seed's transformation from a tiny entity to a giant shade-bearing tree, businesses often start as small, humble ideas, only to evolve over time through consistent effort and nurturing.

Many of the world's renowned entrepreneurs—like Steve Jobs, Jeff Bezos, or Elon Musk—didn't start with vast stores of resources. Instead, they began with an idea, a passion, a 'seed' if you will, which they tirelessly cultivated. They leveraged their most significant assets—creativity, perseverance, and an unwavering belief in their vision—to fuel their fledgling ventures.

As an entrepreneur, embracing this reality forms the backbone of your journey. It serves as a reminder that huge success can come from humble beginnings. Nurturing your idea is just as essential as having that idea in the first place.

9.2. The Power of Patience and Perseverance

There's another crucial lesson to learn here—one of patience and perseverance. A mustard seed doesn't grow to be a large tree overnight. It requires constant nurturing, adequate sunlight, fertile soil—the right conditions to slowly germinate and mature over time.

Likewise, your business won't burgeon immediately. Building a brand, establishing a customer base, designing and improving products and services, requires tireless effort, a resilience against failures and setbacks, and most importantly, an enduring patience that can survive the most challenging times. Humility, tolerance, perseverance—these potent qualities are paramount for the entrepreneur, as they were for Jesus in his time.

9.3. Nurture Your Seed: Developing Your Vision

As an entrepreneur, your vision is your seed. It's the foundation upon which every decision, strategy, and business plan is built. The mustard seed, though being the smallest, grows into a garden's largest plant. Similarly, your vision, while it may start small, has the potential to influence millions.

Gather around you a team of people who believe in your vision, nurture it with solid business acumen, industriousness, and an unwavering commitment to your customers' needs. Like a diligent gardener tending to their crops, weigh each step with its implications—how it aligns with your vision, the impact on your customers, and the influence on your team. Nurture your vision with care, compassion, and consistency, and watch it thrive.

9.4. A Safe Haven for Many: The Larger Purpose

The mustard seed's journey does not end at becoming the tallest plant in the garden. Its ultimate purpose is to serve as a safe haven, a nourishing space that offers protection and supports life.

In the same vein, your entrepreneurial journey must not only be centered on profit or expansion but also on enabling, empowering, and improving the lives of customers, employees, and the community at large. Companies that prioritize purpose as much as profit often experience a greater degree of success, as they're no longer merely selling a product or service—they're enriching lives.

9.5. A Leap of Faith: Trusting the Divine Plan

Faith, in mere size comparable to a grain of mustard seed, can move mountains - Jesus once said. As an entrepreneur, your journey will be laden with uncertainties, tough decisions, and moments of self-doubt. But this is where faith plays its role. Not just in the spiritual sense, but faith in your abilities, in your vision, and the positivity of your actions.

There will be times when logic might fail and the path forward may seem blurred. But the unwavering faith in your mission and the courage to persevere through adversities is what eventually leads to growth—much like the mustard seed that braves the odds to become a mighty tree.

The parable of the mustard seed is a powerful metaphor for entrepreneurs. While the world of entrepreneurship seems complicated, this chapter serves as a reminder of how Jesus' teaching simplifies it. The businesses that last are not necessarily those that start with the most resources, but those that weather the challenges of growth, nurture their vision, serve a purpose, and above all, have an unyielding faith in their mission. If there's something to take from the powerful parable of the mustard seed—no beginning is too small, no dream too big, and no journey too complicated when armed with unwavering faith and unyielding perseverance.

Chapter 10. The Loaves and Fishes: Maximizing Limited Resources

In the Gospel of Matthew, we encounter the enchanting narrative of Jesus feeding a multitude by miraculously multiplying five loaves and two fish. This historical parable brims with wisdom, lessons, and teachings that serve as a solid beacon of light for today's entrepreneurs, especially in resource management.

10.1. Understanding the Parable

In the hot and arduous desert, a massive crowd had gathered around Jesus to listen to his teachings. As the day began to wane, the disciples realized that the throng of people hadn't eaten, and urged Jesus to send them away to nearby towns for food. Jesus, however, saw an opportunity to teach a lesson. He asked his disciples to feed the crowd. All they had at their disposal were five loaves of bread and two fish - apparently not enough to feed five thousand men, let alone women and children.

In the midst of this resource crunch, Jesus prayed, blessed the humble food, broke the bread, and gave it, along with the fish, to his disciples to distribute. To their surprise, everyone ate and was satisfied, and there was an excess, to the extent of twelve baskets-full of leftovers.

10.2. Key Entrepreneurial Lessons

The story relayed above underscores the power of optimism, faith and resourcefulness, which are valuable virtues in the world of entrepreneurship. The act of Jesus feeding the multitude symbolizes how effective resource management, coupled with unwavering faith, can turn a scarcity situation into one of abundance.

From this parable, several entrepreneurial lessons emerge:

1. Start with What You Have: The disciples started with just five loaves and two fish. Everything you need to start or grow your business might already be within your reach: your talents, networks, ideas or personal values. Identify these resources and begin there.

2. Cultivate an Optimistic Mindset: Jesus did not see scarcity in five loaves and two fish; he saw potential. In business, maintaining a positive outlook, even in the face of adversity, is critical.

3. Faith and Action: The disciples believed in Jesus and followed His instruction. In your entrepreneurial journey, showing faith in your vision and combining it with action steps is vital.

4. Proper Management of Resources: No matter how limited, effective resource management can work wonders. Jesus showcased a sense of orderliness and discipline that entrepreneurs need to harness fully.

5. Creative Problem-Solving: Jesus' innovative yet simple solution to a pressing problem teaches us that there are often unexplored ways to solve a challenge. Be creative and explore unorthodox solutions.

6. Value to the Community: Jesus provided value to the community, aligning with the essence of entrepreneurship, which is creating value.

7. Harvest the Abundance: There were twelve baskets of leftovers, demonstrating that effective leadership and resource management can lead not just to sufficiency, but also to abundance.

10.3. Implementing the Lessons

Now that we've discussed the key entrepreneurial lessons derived from this parable, it's time to look at how they can be implemented in practical business scenarios.

10.4. Maximise Existing Resources

Sitting in the face of scarcity, entrepreneurs often tend to focus on what they don't have rather than what they do have. Resourcefulness is all about maximising the utility of existing resources.

10.5. Foster a Culture of Innovation

Creativity and innovation play a significant role in effective resource management. In your entrepreneurial journey, always be open to new ideas that would allow you to maximize limited resources.

10.6. Build a Community

Remember the crowd that witnessed the miracle unfold? As an entrepreneur, your task is to create products or services that provide a solution to your community. When you focus on giving, returns come naturally.

10.7. Embrace Abundance

Abundance is a mindset, not a bank account figure. When you believe in making the very most out of what you have, and have faith in your abilities, you'll experience the abundance that the disciples witnessed with those twelve baskets of leftovers.

The narrative of the loaves and fishes is a compelling metaphor for businesses today. As you navigate your entrepreneurial journey, remember these lessons, and watch as scarcity turns to surplus, adversity to advantage, and trials to triumphs. Keep the faith, stay determined, and emulate the lessons learned from this parable: That's the key to unlocking the potential within you and your entrepreneurial venture.

Chapter 11. Jesus and Communication: Creating Impactful Interactions

To understand the relationship between Jesus' teachings and impactful business communication, one must first delve deeply into the nuanced ways in which Jesus communicated. His means and methods of speaking, teaching, and demonstrating his principles provide a treasure trove of lessons for today's entrepreneurs.

11.1. The Basis of Successful Communication: Love and Respect

At the heart of Jesus' communication style was a deep sense of love and respect for every individual. No matter who he was interacting with — outcasts, sinners, tax collectors, women, children, the sick, or the wealthy — his interactions were always marked by genuine care. In today's business landscape, this translates into treating every stakeholder — be it colleagues, employees, clients, stakeholders, or competition — with utmost respect. When a leader cultivates an atmosphere of dignity and mutual respect, it facilitates open and honest communication, which is instrumental in nurturing resilient entrepreneurial ecosystems.

11.2. Listening: A Forgotten Skill

Jesus was an exemplary listener. Even when he was surrounded by thousands of followers, he made time to listen to individual concerns. He gave people his undivided attention, demonstrated empathy, and validated their feelings. Entrepreneurs need to cultivate this essential skill of deep listening. By truly hearing the needs, ideas, and feedback of their team and customers, innovative ideas can be birthed, potential crisis averted and strong relationships built.

11.3. Parables: Art of Storytelling

Jesus was a master storyteller. He skillfully used parables — simple, relatable stories — to communicate complex, abstract concepts. These stories formed lasting impressions and made his teachings accessible to all. In an entrepreneurial setting, the art of storytelling can be used to communicate the company's vision, mission, and values. Inspiring stories can galvanize a team, appeal to the emotions of the consumers and build more lasting, authentic connections.

11.4. The Power of Questions

Jesus often used questions to engage his audience, stimulate thinking, and foster self-reflection. His questions were neither confrontational nor disdainful but posed in a manner that encouraged discourse and discovery. Similarly, entrepreneurs can use powerful, open-ended questions to encourage creativity, problem-solving, and critical thinking amongst their teams. Questions can also be used effectively in marketing to engage customers and elicit values and needs to develop relevant products and services.

11.5. Clarity and Simplicity

Jesus' teachings are renowned for their crystal-clear clarity and simplicity. He did not use complicated language or indulge in intellectual verbosity. His messages were direct and easily comprehended. Businesses can benefit from embracing this principle, maintaining transparency, and communicating in straightforward language that everyone can understand unambiguously.

11.6. Non-Verbal Communication

Jesus' non-verbal communication— his actions, facial expressions, and how he treated people — spoke louder than words. His compassionate actions reflected his teachings of love, forgiveness, and service. In a business setting, actions indeed speak louder than words. A leader's actions — how they treat their employees, how transparent they are in their dealings, how they handle crisis or make tough decisions — echo through the organization louder than any motivational talk or written mission statements.

11.7. The Authenticity Factor

Jesus embodied authenticity. There was no disparity between what he said and what he did. In the world of business, authenticity breeds trust, and trust is the cornerstone of impactful business relationships. Entrepreneurs must ensure their actions align with their words and promises to build lasting bonds with clients, partners, and employees.

As we dissect and digest these communication principles that Jesus modeled, it is evident that they extend beyond time, culture, and circumstance. They serve as beacons of timeless wisdom that, when applied, can embellish the entrepreneurial journey with integrity, empathy, and meaningful success. The opportunity to learn from this ultimate teacher is ours for the taking, especially when the lessons gleaned have a tempo tuned to the rhythm of both our personal and professional lives.

Chapter 12. Gethsemane and Passion: Resilience in the Face of Challenges

In the heart of Jerusalem, surrounded by ancient olive trees, lies the Garden of Gethsemane - a landmark of immense significance, especially for the Christian faith. This was the place where Jesus Christ spent time in thoughtful prayer and registered remarkable resilience just before the charged ordeal of his Passion. The lessons from Gethsemane have immense value for entrepreneurs today, particularly in understanding the importance of resilience in the face of challenges.

12.1. The Garden in Context

Gethsemane, in the eyes of the entrepreneur, is a powerful metaphor that illustrates the grueling ordeal one might face in a business cycle. Often, entrepreneurial endeavors carry an element of risk, a fear of loss, a great deal of uncertainty, and a likely encounter with stress and anguish. This mirrors the emotional struggle Jesus bore in the Garden.

One could argue that it is at Gethsemane where Jesus' divine resilience is most starkly illustrated. In the face of impending challenges, Jesus prays, "Abba, Father, all things are possible for you. Take this cup away from me; yet, not what I want, but what you want" (Mark 14:36). In this moment, Jesus is shown asking God for deliverance from his impending suffering, yet he reaffirms his acceptance of God's will rather than his own.

Entrepreneurs too might find themselves in their personal 'Gethsemane' at certain stages of their business— when faced with trials and uncertainties, or critical decisions that could make or break their enterprises. In these times of trials, it is resilience, faith, and acceptance of the outcome that can guide them through.

12.2. Resilience: A Biblical Perspective

Resilience is an essential trait for success, not just in business but in all aspects of life. It's the quality that enables us to withstand and bounce back from adversity and carry on with a positive outlook. The Bible presents many stories and teachings that implicitly highlight this virtue and its transformative power.

Jesus' actions in the Garden demonstrate this resilience beautifully. Despite knowing the suffering that awaited him, Jesus prayed for the strength to endure the test ahead. Faced with a moment of profound difficulty, he found the strength to pray, to seek connection with God, and to surrender to a will greater than his own. This lesson certainly carries significance for entrepreneurs facing their own challenging 'Gethsemane' moments.

12.3. Demonstrating Resilience in Business

Resilience does not mean the absence of suffering or the ability to prevent challenging circumstances. It refers to our ability to deal with them. This is best exemplified in Jesus' prayer in the garden. In the face of unimaginable future suffering, Jesus demonstrated acceptance and readiness to bear the cup given to him. This act formed the basis of resilience inherent in the tales of Gethsemane, which has a profound message for entrepreneurs: resilience means having the strength and faith to confront any challenge head-on and continue the journey.

Beyond passive acceptance, resilience requires a proactive approach towards problem-solving and decision-making. In biblical context, Jesus, though seeking deliverance, prepared himself for the impending agony. For today's entrepreneur, this may translate into acknowledging the approaching storm, strategizing to overcome it, and courageously facing whatever may come their way.

12.4. Faith and Resilience

Faith serves as a bedrock for the infusion of resilience during tough times. Entrepreneurship, in particular, is an ever-volatile journey with constant ups and downs. However, holding onto a steadfast belief — be it in a higher power, in one's mission, or in the power of resilience — can be an entrepreneur's strongest anchor point. Jesus, on the way to the cross, showed faith in a higher mission, the divine will, and in turn, awakened resilience, perseverance, and courage to face whatever lay ahead.

12.5. Application for the Modern Entrepreneur

The teachings from Gethsemane provide some profound insights for the entrepreneurial mindset. There will be times of hardship, despair and immense pressure, but the spirit of resilience that we witness in Jesus' time at Gethsemane, can guide us, too. No matter how dire the circumstance, an infallible commitment to the vision and an unswerving faith in the mission can move mountains.

Most importantly, being an entrepreneur is not just about surviving the storm; it's about learning, growing, and spiritually evolving from these experiences. Entrepreneurs should remember that hardships are a part of every journey and are often opportunities destined to refine and perfect us.

In conclusion, resilience is the unspoken hero of the Gethsemane narrative and a vital character trait for successful entrepreneurs. It is the essence of faith, the perseverance in the face of adversity, and the acceptance of trials as pathways to growth. It is the quiet confidence that, in spite of all we fear and withstand, we shall ultimately overcome. Remember, every dark night has a bright dawn that follows, and every Gethsemane has its resurrection.

Chapter 13. The Resurrection: Turning Failure into Success

Even in the gloomiest hours of his life, having been rejected and vilified by the very people he came to save, crucified on the cross, Jesus demonstrated an extraordinary willpower that eventually led to his resurrection. This captivating story serves as an inspiring guide for entrepreneurs facing failures in their endeavors. It illustrates how the most tormenting difficulties can catalyze profound transformation, leading us ultimately to triumph.

13.1. Trading Defeat for Victory

The crucifixion of Jesus, a picture of ultimate despair, was paradoxically the prelude to the greatest victory in history. After his death, he was resurrected, proving the supreme power of faith. Similarly, entrepreneurial journey is also fraught with moments of failure and disappointment. A start-up might go under, or a new product may receive negative reviews, at times leaving the entrepreneur in a state of despair. However, just like Jesus, entrepreneurs can also rise from the ashes of defeat, transforming their failures into success. This transformation starts with an unwavering faith in their mission and conviction in their capabilities.

A failed venture doesn't have to signal the end of the road. Instead, it can be a invaluable lesson, a stepping stone towards success. The key is to exhibit resilience, commitment, and purpose, and to remain unwavering in the face of difficulties.

13.2. The Power of Resilience

Resilience is a crucial attribute most of successful entrepreneurs share. Faced with physical torment and the weight of the world's sins, Jesus still chose to carry out his mission through to the end. His resilience in the face of harrowing adversity is an emblem of fortitude that every entrepreneur must emulate.

Like Jesus, entrepreneurs are required to be resilient. They often face numerous challenges that can derail their projects or mar their vision. This is especially true in the initial stages of a new business venture when the entrepreneur has to bear multiple pressures such as financial insecurity, challenges in team-building, and competitors' hostility. By building resilience, entrepreneurs can brace themselves to withstand these pressures, while steadfastly advancing towards accomplishing their goals.

13.3. Reframing Failure

Reacting to failures in a constructive light is also crucial. Rather than wallowing in despair, entrepreneurs must learn to reframe their failures as opportunities to learn and grow. Jesus' resurrection from the depths of despair teaches us that even in the darkest hours, the potential for rebirth and resurgence always exists.

When a venture falls flat or an idea doesn't take off, instead of viewing it as a failure, entrepreneurs should approach it as an opportunity to study what went wrong, why it happened, and how to improve upon the shortcomings. The wisdom and lessons gained from these times of distress, if used resourcefully, can serve as stepping stones to success.

13.4. Ethical Leadership

The resurrection also highlights Jesus' principles of ethical leadership. Despite undergoing intense suffering, he did not sway from his mission and his commitment to his followers. He showcased transparent communication, integrity, and humility throughout his life, which only strengthened after his resurrection. Ethical leadership is crucial in the world of entrepreneurship, where leaders guide the vision of their organizations and play key roles in shaping their organizational culture.

An entrepreneur who adopts these ethical leadership principles builds trust within their team, boosting overall morale and productivity. In the long run, this kind of leadership results in sustainable, ethical businesses.

The story of Jesus' resurrection symbolizes the power of perseverance and renewal amidst hardship and adversity. By embodying these lessons, entrepreneurs can pave the way to success through even the most challenging hurdles.